CW00498337

ON READING

Provocations, consolations &
suggestions for reading more freely

Nick Parker

{ TXT EDITIONS }

First published November 2020
by That Explains Things Ltd.

Copyright © 2020 Nick Parker

Illustration also copyright © 2020 Nick Parker

All rights reserved. You can't reprint or reproduce this
book in any form at all without permission from me.
(Except for quotes and that.)

The moral rights of the author have been asserted.
(We had a great big 'asserting ceremony' with chanting.)

A limited edition hardback is also available (until
they're all gone). To get one of those as well, go to:
www.thatexplainsthings.com/on-reading

For George and Laurie.
Every book is a universe. You'll see.

How do you read?

IN ONE WAY or another, I've spent a life with books: I studied English and Philosophy at university; I've worked in bookshops and in publishing; I've written and edited books; my house looks like it's built out of bookshelves; and it's a running joke that in any given conversation I'll invariably say 'that reminds me of a thing I read recently...'

I remember at primary school, once you'd finished all the reading scheme books, you were allowed to choose any book you liked from the library. It was called 'being a free reader'.

And yet for a long time as an adult, I didn't feel like a 'free reader' at all: I read slowly, fitfully, forgetfully. Too often I seemed to make reading a chore, reading books because I felt I ought to, rather than because I wanted to. I rarely got 'lost in a book' the way I remembered from childhood. And I seemed to lack the ability to see a book through – abandoning most of them about a third of the way in. I felt like there was a knack to being a 'proper reader' and that somehow I didn't quite have it.

Over time, I began to see more clearly that my difficulties were because of certain assumptions and hang-ups I'd been putting in my own way. And as I began to articulate these to myself, it all started to come a little more easily. I even did little personal 'experiments in reading' for my own amusement.

Fast forward to a few months ago. Someone I didn't know on Twitter asked 'what tips do people have for reading more books?' and by the time I'd hit reply for the seventh or eighth time it was obvious the question had uncorked something in me. I kept with the theme in a weekly newsletter I write, which got a flood of replies all essentially saying the same thing: *I've never really thought about how I read before. Now I have, it turns out I've got all kinds of weird habits going on!*

This little book started in that newsletter, has grown in conversations over a few months, and is offered here as a collection of consolations, provocations and suggestions for anyone else who feels they need a bit of help reading more freely.

Nick Parker
October 2020

Sacred and profane

For what it's worth: I studied English and Philosophy, then worked in a bookshop, then in publishing. All places where books are treated both as 'sacred objects of contemplation' and 'logistical problems in need of managing'. That's a useful tension, I think.

Penguins and snakes

QUICK BOOKSHOP story to make bibliophiles weep: Penguin books used to avoid the hassle of processing 'returns' (shops sending back unsold books every quarter) by asking you to tear off the covers, return those, and then throw away the rest of the books. The first time I stood in the basement of a bookshop ripping off the covers of a pile of Penguin Classics I genuinely felt sick.

Mind you, the same week my mate Andy got a job in a zoo, where he had to sit all day in a room smacking mice on the head with a hammer so they became snake food. So, y'know. Perspective.

Buy the damn book

HAVE LOTS of interesting books around. To help with this: always buy the book. In the scheme of things, books cost nothing. The equivalent of a couple of pints. Less than a pizza.

If you're broke and can't afford books, you'll know. If you're feeling like 'Hmm, I'm not sure whether I should or not...' Yes, you should. Buy the damn book.

My sense is that we prevaricate about buying books, not because of the cost, but because the feeling of having 'too many' unread books around weighs on us in some way.

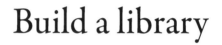

Build a library

IF IT HELPS, tell yourself and others, 'I'm building a library'.

I used to say this as a joke.

It's not a joke.

Fuel

THE PHYSICAL presence of books can feel like such a responsibility, can't it? Especially if you're in the habit of BUYING THE DAMN BOOK. Overwhelmed bookshelves; angry significant others; a burdensome weight. I think it helps to give away, donate or even recycle books regularly. It clears physical space for more books. And it clears the mind a little, too.

I once met a long-retired vicar who told me that back when he first 'answered the call', if someone in his parish died, their family would invariably give him their dead relative's Bible. He tended a big parish; he was given a lot of Bibles.

So, he said, he'd stack them up in the cellar of the vicarage, and in the winter he'd use them as fuel for the stove.

Oh, God's Word might be sacred, he said, but don't confuse that with what's just paper and ink.

Amen to that. (I think.)

Know your limits

Know your own self-limiting reading habits. If you read according to principles like 'I've started this book, so I must finish it' or 'Don't start a new book until you've finished the one you're on', just stop it.

You wouldn't consume any other medium like this ('Must complete this whole website before I click on anything else!').

Put the boring book down and pick up another. The sense of obligation is entirely imagined. Nobody will judge you and nothing bad will happen.

Hurl

No, we can do better than simply 'putting the boring book down'. Make stopping reading feel as decisive as starting reading.

Have a specific place on your bookshelf for 'books I stopped reading' – and perhaps even another for 'books that are on a bit of a time out'.

If you're really fed up with a book, hurl it across the room or out of a window. It's very cathartic.

(I once got so angry with a book that I got out of my chair, walked straight to my local charity shop and gave it away. Then a few days later I felt bad that someone else might unwittingly buy it without realising what they were getting into, so I went back to the shop, bought it back, wrote exactly what I thought of the book in felt tip, then re-donated it again.)

Guru

JAMES CLEAR, who's an expert on how to form new habits successfully, sums all this up more constructively: 'Start more books, quit most of them, read the great ones twice.'

Gift

ENTERTAIN the idea of never lending out a book again. Instead – give them away, then buy yourself a replacement. A lent book often lingers in the background of a friendship as a little irritating obligation. (When will they return it? Will they have folded the corners down?) Whereas a gift is a gift is a gift.

THINK OF BOOKS not just as objects but as a ceaseless nourishing flow of words through your life. Pay as much attention to the texture and quality of the ebbing and flowing as much as the individual books.

Tortoise

DON'T GET hung up on whether you read fast or slow. Those apps that read books to you faster so you can cram more words into your head, 'like Warren Buffet, Elon Musk and other CEOs' (?!) are all hare. Reading more –and more deeply – is all tortoise.

Forget it

DON'T GET hung up on remembering and recall, either. It all goes in one way or another, whether you think you can remember it or not.

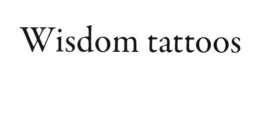

Wisdom tattoos

ALTHOUGH IT is nice to make some notes shortly after reading a book. It doesn't so much help you remember more as notice more. So write a summary, or identify a few of your favourite paragraphs and copy them out long-hand into a good notebook. It feels like you're tattooing wisdom onto your very soul.

ALTHOUGH, despite what you might have read recently, you're not actually tattooing wisdom onto your soul. You'll forget stuff just the same. Most of it, in fact.

But browsing and re-reading a notebook of favourite paragraphs is, in itself, one of the most pleasurable types of reading there is.

Read with a pencil

WRITE IN your books. I know for some, marking books feels like sacrilege. For others it's too much like 'study'. I think of it as an ongoing conversation with the author – noting where you agree or disagree; expressing what thoughts, feelings or tangents your reading inspires, right there in the moment.

You are in fine company: many writers are prolific scribblers of marginalia, and any number of works started out as an underlined thought or angrily inked comment around the edges of another author's book.*

In fact, writing in books is such a fruitful way of sparking ideas and exploring your own thoughts that, as author and artist Austin Kleon points out, if you want to be a writer you must first be a reader – but the next crucial step is 'becoming a reader with a pencil'.

---

*For more on marginalia, google 'The Marginal Obsession with Marginalia' by Mark O'Connell from the 26th January 2012 issue of *The New Yorker*. (Ideally, print it out and write your thoughts about the piece around the edges as you go...)

Piles

HAVE LOTS of books on the go. How many?
How many places can you get away with making small piles of books? One pile by the bed,
another on the desk, a book or two in my ruck-
sack, a small stack by the comfy chair...

Talking among themselves

ALTERNATIVELY, let the books themselves tell you how many to read at the same time. The novelist Richard Powers says he finds having one fiction and one non-fiction book on the go at the same time lets the two books 'triangulate against each other and conjure up some third space'.

I like this idea that the books you're reading are 'in conversation' with each other. And, of course, there are different flavours of conversation, aren't there?

Reading from each book on a different day is like a thoughtful discussion between friends; reading alternate chapters from each in the same sitting is more like an animated debate with someone you've just met at a party; piling all your books on a desk and reading a paragraph from each creates a sort of mad collage that's more like an unruly panel show. Try them all.

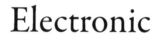

Electronic

EBOOKS are amazing: they improve accessibility, they increase the amount of books you can carry around and they're great if you live in a small place. But I've noticed over time that the memories of books I've read on my Kindle tend to mulch together. Apparently there's science to this*.

Because reading is a recent human invention, we've had to co-opt bits of our brains that evolved for other things – and the bits we use for reading were originally used for spatial awareness. Which is why, when you're hunting for a passage in a book, you can have a strong sense of it being 'on the right hand side, nearly at the bottom'.

I'm not sure what the implications are here. But I do know that it's a good excuse not to tidy one's books: 'Don't touch! That's my memory piled up there.'

---

*It's obligatory that every book must now contain a reference to the neuroscience-of-whatever-it-is-the-book-is-about.

Convenient
bundles

HERE'S SOMETHING liberating: consider that the 'unit of reading' is not the book. It's the chapter. Books are just convenient ways of keeping chapters around the house in neat bundles.

Go smaller

ALTHOUGH WHY stop at chapters? You could decide that your ideal unit of reading is the paragraph.

In fact, in his book *A Few Short Sentences About Writing*, Verlyn Klinkenborg makes a convincing case for the sentence being where it's at. Too often, he says, we treat sentences as though they're to be looked through, in order to 'see' the meaning beyond. But 'what if the virtue, the value of the sentence is the sentence itself and not its extractable meaning?'

For a while after encountering Klinkenborg, I found that paying close attention to just a few sentences a day could be as satisfying as finishing whole books.

Count the ways

Cultivate different ways of reading: slow mulling-over reading in a comfy chair. Fast skim-reading sitting at your desk. Easy fall-asleep reading before bed. Quick 'grab an idea' reading before going for a walk.

Make these different ways of reading real and distinct by giving them names, like they're yoga moves. Now mix them up. Try different styles of reading with different types of books.

Mind commuting

A THING I just remembered: a few years ago I stopped commuting into London and started working from a shed at the end of my garden. Accordingly, my commute shrank from 90 minutes each morning to about thirty seconds.

For a while I reserved what had previously been my commuting time for reading. It was blissful. Over an hour of 'guilt-free' reading every morning while my mind was fresh, the house was quiet and the world wasn't yet pinging me emails.

After a few months, work got busier and I stopped. But now I've remembered it, I'm going to reinstate 'mind commuting'. Even if just for 15 minutes at the start and end of every working day.

It's a date

WITH THAT in mind, book 30-minute slots into your work calendar for reading. (Call them things like '*Catch-up w/Dostoevsky re: Project Karamazov*'.)

Life story

A FRIEND of mine tells a story about when he was 17 or 18 and getting into reading magazines like *National Geographic* and *The Economist*. He got up from the kitchen table one day saying, 'Anyway, I need to catch up on my reading.'

To which his mother answered, without looking up: 'Welcome to the rest of your life.'

Craving

I ONCE READ an article about someone trying to give up smoking. The author said the moment she knew she needed to give up was when she realised she kept at least five packets of cigarettes at all times: one in her coat pocket, one in her bag, another in the glove box of the car, one on her desk, and an emergency pack in her filing cabinet.

How awful to be so enslaved to an addiction like that. Also: No, I never thought of keeping a book in the car either!

Pockets

ONLY BUY a coat once you've ascertained that a B-format paperback will fit in the pocket.

Do it with others

READ IN COMPANY. Every year I go on a 'reading weekend' – a group of seven or eight of us in a large house, with a selection of books (we all recommend five) laid out on a big table, and three rules: take one book from the table at a time; read between meals; talk over meals.

Rob Poynton, whose idea this was, says the books are there as stimuli for interesting conversations. That may be so, but the experience of collective reading is absolutely addictive. It's completely different to reading alone: in the company of others, I have a different quality of attention; I can read for hours without a break; I notice more. It's completely electrifying.

Indulge, radically

YES, AS IT happens, I *do* feel slightly self-conscious talking about going on a 'reading weekend'. Making reading the main thing seems like such a radically indulgent idea.

When I tell people about these weekends in conversation, I often notice a flicker of something cross their face, and I start to think I've just admitted something taboo.

I'm usually thinking this while they've moved on to talking about their entirely normal weekends walking up a hill and down again, or travelling halfway across the country to hit a tiny ball around a massive field, or sitting on a beach doing absolutely nothing at all.

Join

I've been in a few book clubs over the years. Reading a book knowing you'll be discussing it with others makes for a pleasingly different experience of reading. I find it's a particularly good way of spending time with books you don't like.

But always judge a book club by the rules it uses for picking the books.

The best book club I was ever in had the rule: *Pick a book you've long been meaning to read but haven't got round to.* The 'long been meaning to' meant we avoided chasing trends; 'haven't got round to' meant we were never reading anyone's best-loved book. Nobody ever felt like they needed to defend their choice. In fact, there was always something energising about finding you hated the book you'd chosen.

Book clubs where people pick their favourite books in the hope that everyone else will love them too are actually death cults and will destroy your friendships. Avoid.

Aloud

READ OUT LOUD. To yourself. To other people. To passing dogs and cats. Tricky passages offer up their meaning; dull paragraphs spring to life. Books are musical and too often we forget to tune in.

A contemplative dozen

I REMEMBER hearing the jazz pianist and teacher David Sudnow get asked what new music he recommended his students listen to. He replied that, in truth, he only really listened to the same dozen or so albums, as they contained everything he needed.

I'm not sure the same thing holds true for books. But the idea of one's reading being a sort of 'quest for the dozen or so books that might make up one's own library of contemplation' feels like it adds a pleasing extra dimension to a reading life.

Paper Museum

Every Christmas, in lieu of a greetings card, the writer Ian Sansom used to send out a little booklet called the Paper Museum. It consisted of 52 extracts from books he'd read that year – books he'd reviewed, books he'd bought, books he'd encountered in libraries, favourites he'd re-read. Fiction, poetry, philosophy, articles from newspapers or magazines, anything and everything.

This seems to me to be the perfect companion to a reading life – not least because of the constant small pleasure of being able to mull over the question 'is this one for the Paper Museum?' And then! To have a record of one's reading year captured so beautifully.

They weren't particularly fancy things. A5 in size, simply typeset; totally achievable with modest word processing skills and a stapler. Perhaps we should all build our own Paper Museums.

Whim

ANYWAY, I called Mr Sansom to check I'd got my facts straight about the Paper Museum. He said yes, that was about the size of it, and added that it had all started when he first encountered a university library, where he would wander the endless open stacks, plucking books entirely at random.

Like some kind of idiotic hack, I found myself asking him what his 'top 3 tips were for improving one's reading'. He said:

One: Read at whim.

Two: Read at whim.

Three: Read at whim.

Mr S also said something about preferring books to people, and a book being like a faithful dog, or perhaps that reading was a bit like taking a dog out for a walk, but if I'm honest my attention had wandered because I was trying to remember the Groucho Marx quote about books and dogs: '*Outside of a dog, a book is a man's best friend. Inside of a dog, it's too dark to see.*'

Which I think we can all agree just about sums things up.

Worth

A FRIEND ONCE said all she needed from a book is 'one thing, and that's enough. One idea. One description that really puts its finger on something. One connection to something new. One good joke.'

Somehow, I found that very liberating. I think before then, I'd slipped into a habit of assuming that every book had to be an absolute life-changing humdinger, and I'd start getting restless if it wasn't shaping up that way.

Toilet

CONSIDER the 'toilet book'. Notice how we've taken a specific moment – sitting on the loo with a few minutes of idle attention spare – and created a genre of book around it.

I wonder if we could do this for other times and places?

Books that fit in cutlery drawers so you can dip into them while waiting for the kettle to boil. Books that'll stay put on car dashboards for reading at traffic lights. Books that slide easily under pillows for reading to one's lover in the small hours.

Telly

My FANTASY intellectual self doesn't own a television and spends his evenings reading and contemplating. My real self likes Netflix and vegging out in front of a box set.

Not long ago, I had a small epiphany: it doesn't have to be all or nothing. You can choose to read in an evening – for the length of a TV programme.

So now, some evenings, I'll watch something on TV with my wife, then I'll go off and read for an hour while she watches something I'm not into, then we'll finish the evening watching something else together.

Thumb

PUT YOUR e-reader app where your Twitter / Facebook / Instagram app currently lives on your phone.

Behemoth

GOT A Big Literary Behemoth you've been meaning to read for years, but somehow it's never quite the right time for *War and Peace*, *Infinite Jest* or Proust? Make a deliberate decision to read it slowly. Very slowly. A single page a day. That way you can carry on with the rest of your reading life as normal, and not feel guilty that you're not making 'enough progress' with the Big Book.

I got this idea from a friend who took four years to read Hilary Mantel's *Wolf Hall* when her kids were little. She said once she gave herself over to the idea of reading it slowly, she luxuriated in it, savoured every sentence.

(And if I'd heeded this advice when she told me, I'd be within a hair's breadth of finishing *Ulysses* by now.)

Constant

'Avid reader.' 'Voracious reader.' 'Prolific reader.' These are labels that non-readers use to describe people who read a lot. I don't like them.

They have a sort of breathless energy that, for me, isn't at all like the experience of reading. They're descriptions that seem overly impressed with the quantity or pace of reading; they're wrong in the same way as saying someone has a 'wacky' sense of humour. This says more about the person who says it than the other person's sense of humour.

I read two or three books a week but I can't say I feel avid, prolific or voracious. 'Regular' or 'constant' is probably more like it. 'Omnivorous' or 'eclectic' would be nice. But 'patchy' or 'undisciplined' are fine too, to be honest.

Relationships

NOTICE THE different types of relationships you have with books. We often slip into letting books take the position of authority. (A friend of mine, an otherwise confident and daring creative artist, always says he can't help 'playing low status' to books.)

I recently met Edward Espé Brown, a Zen priest, cook and writer. He said he was noticing more often these days how he seems to turn to his books as friends and helpers. 'I can ask them a question and open a book, and it'll be like, oh, thank you friend. That's interesting. Yes, that's exactly what I need to hear.'

(Though to be fair, 'finding what you need by looking exactly where you are' is kinda the Zen superpower, isn't it?)

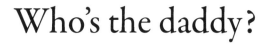

Who's the daddy?

WHAT TO read next? Now, there's a question. I like to let the book I'm reading now suggest the one that might follow – often explicitly, if the author references another book or writer; sometimes implicitly ('what book naturally seems to follow from this one?'). I like the feeling of eternally hopping from one book to the next, to the next, to the next.

Another variant on this theme that I like is to think which books are the 'parents' of this one? (From any of the current crop of life-hacking self-help books, hop back to *Feel the Fear and Do it Anyway*, then hop to *How to Win Friends and Influence People*, and just a couple more hops will get you to Aristotle's *Ethics**.) That sense of 'oh, *this* is how these books fit together' is likely the essence of what it means to be a 'discerning reader'.

---

*It's astonishing how often you'll end up back at Aristotle. And to be fair, philosophers have long 'joked' that the history of Western thought is basically 'footnotes to Plato'. (And yes, I am inordinately pleased that this is now also a footnote about footnotes to Plato.)

Clusters *of* expertise

OR, IF YOU'VE had enough of all this whimsy and are hoping for at least one *productivity-optimising reading hack* before it's all over, you might prefer an approach more like Slava Akhmechet's. He's not a hopper. He's much more focused. He'd say *cluster* and become an expert.

He reasons thus: if you read one book on a topic then you'll know more about that subject than almost everyone else alive (because most people don't read). Now read two books on the same subject and you'll know more than most other readers. And if you read a cluster of the five best books on any subject, chances are you'll acquire a fresh way of seeing the world that almost nobody else has.

The key is creating clusters around themes: 'study X subject through Y lens'. Akhmechet points out that it's more fun to make 'Y' something unusual (e.g. 'study failure through the biographies of one-term presidents')*.

---

*For the full explanation of his 'cluster' approach, go to: www.spakhm.com/p/how-i-read

Closure

I USED to find the moment of finishing a book to be a strange anti-climax. In truth, I'd often have been emotionally distancing myself for a fair few pages, preparing for the parting of ways, the end of the affair.

Recently, I've tried to do the opposite. To take the last page or two deliberately slowly, to give my reading a proper sense of *diminuendo*, then to close the covers and spend a few minutes reflecting on what was particularly vivid or interesting, or whatever.

Then I'll take it to a shelf, tuck it into place and say 'thank you' to it. Which sounds absurd as I type it – but, well, it's just what I do.

You can, of course, do whatever you please. We're all free readers, after all.

Thank you

Thanks to @garethkthomas, whose question prompted the newsletter that became this little book. Thanks to Rob Poynton for his excellent suggestions and Extremely High Quality Conversations. Thanks to Sonali Chapman, Eleanor Hill, Edward Espé Brown and Ian Sansom for ideas that became experiments in reading, everyone who responded to the newsletter piece with such enthusiastic thoughts and suggestions, and for everyone at Yellow Learning who gathered to answer the question 'how do you read?' (Sincere apologies to those who then experimented with BUYING THE DAMN BOOK at significant personal cost.) Thanks to Neil Baker, largely because he admitted to checking the acknowledgements of every book he ever picks up on the off-chance his name might appear. And thanks, always, to Sam, for everything. Sorry about all the piles of books everywhere.

.

NICK PARKER has variously been a joke-writer for radio, a cartoonist for Viz, and the staff writer and editor for *The Oldie* magazine. His short story collection, *The Exploding Boy and other tiny tales* was called 'astonishing' by *The Guardian*, which was nice.

These days he runs the writing agency That Explains Things, where he helps clients 'find their voice, tell their stories, and explain their things'.

He also writes a weekly newsletter which he's yet to find a pithy name for. If you liked this, you'll probably like that. Sign up at: www.thatexplainsthings.com/newsletter.

He lives on the outskirts of town.

Printed in Great Britain
by Amazon

11647892R00059